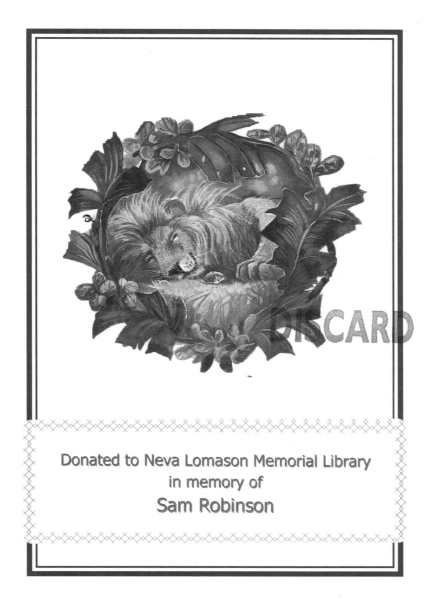

Donated to Neva Lomason Memorial Library
in memory of
Sam Robinson

Aesop's Fables

The Fox and the Grapes
&
Other Fables

 Retold by Andrea Stacy Leach
Illustrated by Holly Hannon

Paradise Press, Inc.

Exclusive distribution by Paradise Press, Inc.
Created and manufactured by arrangement with Ottenheimer Publishers, Inc.
© 1995, 1997 Ottenheimer Publishers, Inc.
All rights reserved. Printed in Italy. SB643A

The Fables

The Fox and the Grapes

The fox was walking along the road when he saw a grapevine growing above him. High off the ground, out of his reach, was a lovely, ripe bunch of grapes.

Now the fox was hungry and thirsty, and he knew the grapes would make a tasty meal. So he jumped up and snapped at the grapes, but he still couldn't reach them.

The fox decided to try a different approach. He stepped back and started to run. When he was under the grapes, he leaped into the air as high as he could . . . but fell to the ground empty-handed.

The fox jumped again and again, but each time, he missed the grapes.

Finally, as hungry and thirsty as ever, he gave up. "I never really wanted those grapes anyway," the fox grumbled as he trotted away. "I am sure they are tough and sour."

It is easy to dislike what you cannot have.

The Grasshopper and the Ants

On a sunny winter day, the ants were busy spreading their grain out to dry. A hungry grasshopper hopped by and asked if they would share their grain. "I am cold, and there is nothing to eat," whined the grasshopper. "All the leaves and grasses are covered with snow."

The ants looked at the grasshopper, shivering in the snow. "Where is your supply of winter food?" they asked. "What did you do all summer while we were busy storing food for the winter?"

"Oh, it was too lovely to work in the summer," the grasshopper said. "I sang all day long."

The ants frowned and went back to work. But one ant turned and said, "Well, if you sang all summer, you will have to dance all winter."

It is better to prepare today for the needs of tomorrow.

The Dog and His Bone

One day the dog stole a big juicy bone from the butcher. As he ran home with his prize, he crossed a small bridge over a stream.

When he stopped and looked down, the dog saw his reflection in the water. He thought his reflection was another dog with a bigger, juicier bone than his.

Now the dog was greedy—so naturally he wanted the bigger bone. He snarled and growled at the other dog.

But as he opened his mouth, his bone fell into the water and was carried away with the stream. So the dog went home with no bone at all.

The greedy are often left with nothing.

The Wolf in Sheep's Clothing

For days the wolf watched the flock of sheep, waiting for a chance to steal a sheep for his dinner. But the shepherd guarded his flock faithfully, and the wolf got hungrier each day.

Then, one day the wolf saw a sheepskin on the ground. He put it over his own fur, and soon he was walking among the sheep unnoticed.

When night came, the shepherd locked the wolf in the pen with the sheep.

"This is the chance I have been waiting for!" the wolf exclaimed, looking for the fattest sheep he could find.

Meanwhile, the shepherd became hungry for supper and walked back to the pen. He reached in and grabbed the first sheep he saw. It was the wolf in sheep's clothing!

Looks can be deceiving.